Phonics

MONSTER

BOOK 4

soft g
soft c
wh th ch
pl fl sh
bl cl
gl sl

sc st sn
squ sp
sk sw sm
tw

pr
tr br
fr cr
gr

scr str
spl spr
thr
kn ph
gn wr

Consonant Blends and Digraphs

Brian Giles   **Joe Ruger**

Table of Contents

Introduction

Phonics Monster - Book 4 offers a comprehensive introduction to Consonant Blends and Consonant Digraphs, as well as silent k and g and soft g and c. This is an "**ESL Phonics**" book, which means that in addition to teaching the various sounds, it focuses on the differences between similar sounds which are especially difficult for ESL students (in contrast with native speakers, to whom such differences are natural).

Consonant "blends" are where two consonants are together, and you say each sound (fl, br, cl, st, tw). Consonant "digraphs" are where two consonants produce a sound that is different from the individual sounds (sh, ch, th, ph).

Sections include:
- Word lists
- Practice sentences
- Rhyming words
- Games
- Reading practice
- Review quiz

Included in the final section is a longer reading passage to help reinforce all of material presented. The Answer Key contains the answers to all of the quizzes and tests.

How to Use This Book

This book contains several word lists and sentences, and it is ideal to begin each lesson by reviewing these. Throughout the book there are also various games. Below are some ideas for making the games more interesting and dynamic in a classroom setting.

Games

The Numbers Game – The Numbers Game consists of several numbered squares that contain a word from the section being taught. The game can be adapted to different formats:
- You, the teacher, call out a word, and the first person to yell out the corresponding number gets a point. The student with the most points is the winner. (The winner could then become the "teacher," and call out words for the other students to find.)
- You, the teacher, call out a word. The first person to yell out the corresponding number then calls out a word for the other students. The first student to call out the number then calls out a number for the rest of the students to find, and so on. (**You may want to "eliminate" the students who have already called out a number, to prevent the same student from winning every time. For example, you can have every student stand up, and when a student correctly calls out the correct number, he or she can then sit down.**)
- Alternatively, you (or a student "teacher") can call out numbers, and the students can yell out the corresponding words.

Bingo – A blank BINGO gameboard is included in 3 of the lessons. Prior to playing, the students must write one word from the word list in that section in each of the squares. (This way, each student will have a unique gameboard.) The teacher then calls out words from the word list, and the students write an **X** over the word (if they have it on their gameboard). The first student to have five **X**'s in a row (vertically, diagonally, or horizontally) is the winner.

Soft g and c – Word Lists

When **g** comes before **e, i,** or **y** (**ge, gi, gy**) it *usually* sounds like a "**j.**" (This is called the **soft g** sound.)

1. gym	rage	huge	cage
2. sage	gem	gist	giant
3. Gen	page	wage	mage
4. gee	genie	sponge	genius

When **c** comes before **e, i,** or **y** (**ce, ci, cy**) it *usually* sounds like an "**s.**" (This is called the **soft c** sound.)

5. mace	nice	cite	cycle
6. mice	lace	race	dice
7. lice	rice	vice	bicycle
8. cell	cent	city	niece

Soft g and c – Sentences

1. The giant will rage in the gym.

2. That is a huge gem!

 3. We race bicycles in the city.

4. Gen's niece likes to race.

5. The mice in the cage are nice.

 6. I will pay one cent for a page.

7. Use the dice to wage a bet.

8. The giant has a cage in the city.

9. The lace looks nice, Gen!

wh can sound like "w," or "hw," and sometimes it sounds like "h."

1. what   whale   when   why

2. wheel   whet   where   who*

3. whack   whole*   while   whiz

4. whoa   wheat   which   white

5. whom*   whine   whose*   whip

*wh sounds like "h."

3

Consonant Digraphs - wh

Sentences

1. Where is the white whale?

2. Why does he whine?

3. Whose wheel is white?

4. Why whack the whip?

5. Who eats whole wheat?

 6. Where is my whip?

7. The wheel is in the wheat.

8. The giant whines in the cage.

Write the word your teacher says on the blanks below. (Answer key in the back of the book.)

1. _____   6. _____

2. _____   7. _____

3. _____   8. _____

4. _____   9. _____

5. _____   10. _____

Listen to the sentences your teacher says, and fill in the blanks with the missing words.

The genie is in a _____ _____.

_____ can _____ on my bike?

Roll the _____ on the _____.

The giant has a _____. He is in a _____.

Review – g / c / wh

Read for Speed

Read the paragraph below, and have your teacher count the seconds. Write your time in the blank below.

Try to read it in **30 seconds**!

If you can't read in 30 seconds, read two more times, and write your times on the blanks below.

> Gen is a giant, but Gen is nice, so Gen's friends say she is a gentle giant. Gen the gentle giant will race her bike to the city to see her niece and get some rice. When Gen rides to the city, she will see huge white mice and yell.
>
> "Whoa!" yells Gen the gentle giant. "White mice in the city!"
>
> "Ha, ha, ha!" say Gen's friends. "You are a giant, and you yell when you see white mice!"

Time 1: _____

Time 2: _____

Time 3: _____

1. ship	shake	shop	wish
2. fish	mash	sheet	shin
3. dash	wash	shun	she
4. shock	dish	sash	shot
5. shoot	shave	shall	mesh
6. shush	sham	Shane	gash
7. bash	gosh	show	shoe
8. cash	hash	posh	shack
9. shame	shine	shone	rash
10. sheep	shut	rush	shade

Consonant Digraphs – sh

Sentences

1. We wash the wet fish.

2. Shane has cash in his shop.

3. Gosh! Don't shock Shane's shin!

4. They eat hash and fish then wash and sleep.

 5. Shame on Shane; he shot a fish.

6. The sheep shall rush to the shade.

7. She has a rash on her shin.

 8. Wash this dish then bake that fish.

9. Where is Gen's cash?

Consonant Digraphs – th

Word List

Aspirated ("with air")

1. thick	tooth	think	thud
2. faith	thin	math	thunder
3. Thor	goth	thing	think
4. bath	cloth	teeth	path

Unaspirated ("without air")

1. this	they	that	those
2. these	there	them	the
3. mother	father	brother	gather

Sentences

1. That cloth is thin.

 2. My father has white teeth.

3. He will take a bath and do his math.

4. They gather the trash on the path.

5. These math books are rather thick.

6. Father has a thin brother.

7. This wheel is thick but that wheel is thin.

8. Put those things in the bath.

Consonant Digraphs – ch / tch
Word List

1. chip	such	chick	lunch
2. chair	much	choose	Chad
3. cheese	chap	teach	chin
4. chase	chime	catch	teacher
5. watch	hatch	fetch	which
6. patch	cheek	kitchen	choke
7. rich	witch	itch	Mitch
8. hitch	pitch	check	match

Consonant Digraphs – ch

Sentences

1. The cheese is in the kitchen.

2. The teacher is not rich.

3. Hot dogs make such a great lunch.

4. Mitch will teach the children math.

5. Chad will watch the match.

6. I have an itch on my cheek.

7. Watch the teacher chase Chad!

8. I will catch if you will pitch.

Consonant Digraphs – sh / th / ch

Review

Practice reading the pairs of words below.

ship / chip	chin / thin
thick / chick	batch / bash
shin / thin	that / chat
math / match	with / witch
thine / shine	thy / shy
much / mush	shoo / chew
bath / bash	patch / path
fish / fitch	ship / chip
chain / Shane	wish / witch
goth / gosh	mash / match
thee / she	chair / there
cheese / these	cash / catch

Consonant Digraphs – sh / th / ch

Numbers Game

Rules (see introduction for more ways to play this game):

- Choose one student to say a word (any word) from below.
- The first student to **find the word** and **say the number** in the box gets to say the next word.

1 chick	2 shake	3 mash	4 bath	5 batch
6 she	7 thee	8 cheap	9 match	10 math
11 rich	12 cash	13 than	14 thine	15 thin
16 shine	17 shin	18 chin	19 chime	20 shape
21 thud	22 check	23 those	24 shun	25 with

Tongue Twisters!

1. Selfish shellfish.

2. Which witch wished which wicked wish?

 ## 3. Six sharp smart sharks.

4. Chop shops stock chops.

5. Chad's big black bath brush broke.

6. Nine nice night nurses nursing nicely.

7. Shy Shelly says she shall sew sheets.

Consonant Digraphs – sh / th / ch

Spelling

Write the word your teacher says on the blanks below. (Answer key in the back of the book.)

1. _____   6. _____

2. _____   7. _____

3. _____   8. _____

4. _____   9. _____

5. _____   10. _____

Listen to the sentences your teacher says, and fill in the blanks with the missing words.

I have a _____ on my _____.

I will _____ the window.

He has a _____ gash on his _____.

There is a _____ by the _____.

*See page 47 for more reading practice.

16

Consonant Blends with l

(bl , fl , sl , gl , cl , pl)

1. black	slow	flat	clap
2. plain	clue	flew	sleep
3. slap	clip	play	float
4. block	flip	glide	plane
5. slip	flock	clean	plant
6. plan	Blake	flap	class
7. bleed	click	flow	blew
8. glow	fled	slight	slay

Consonant Blends with l

Sentences

1. Blake plans to sleep in class.

2. Bob will slide on the sled.

3. We can plant a rose on this block.

4. The big plane flew at night.

5. The flock flies in the sky.

6. Blake has math class on this block.

7. Click on the black plane.

8. Blake, don't slap my cheek!

Consonant Blends with r

(br , cr , dr , fr , gr , pr , tr)

1. broke   crab   drum   free

2. gram   pray   train   Brian

3. creek   drop   Fred   green

4. press   tree   bride   cried

5. drip   grass   prize   friend

6. track   brand   croak   drive

7. frost   groan   trick   brave

8. creep   drove   Grace   prince

Consonant Blends with r

Sentences

1. Grace broke the green drum.

2. Brian will take the free train home.

 3. I pray in bed at night.

4. Frogs croak at the creek all night.

5. The bride grins and cries.

6. If you bleed, be brave.

7. Take a trip in a green train.

8. My friend will trap a crab in the grass.

Consonant Blends with l and r

Review Quiz

Write the word your teacher says on the blanks below. (Answer key in the back of the book.)

1. _____   6. _____

2. _____   7. _____

3. _____   8. _____

4. _____   9. _____

5. _____   10. _____

Listen to the sentences your teacher says, and fill in the blanks with the missing words.

Grace has a _____ for the slum.

Trap the _____ in the pen.

My _____ friend got a _____.

The flock can _____ and _____.

21

Consonant Blends with l and r

Review

Practice reading the pairs of words below.

brake /Blake	clue /crew
free /flee	flat /frat
grew /glue	block /Brock
pray /play	blight /bright
fry /fly	cloak /croak
breed /bleed	blue /brew
crass /class	flow /fro
grad /glad	bled /bred
Fred /fled	glow /grow
crick /click	bloke /broke
Brock /block	glad /grad
frock /flock	clash /crash

Word List

1. stop   stay   stove   fist

2. chest   stale   west   step

3. Stan   stand   stack   store

4. test   steel   gist   still

5. state   study   fast   stool

6. stuck   Steve   steal   stole

7. stove   stick   staff   Stacy

Consonant Blends - st

Sentences

1. Steve will stay in the store.

2. There is a steel stove in the kitchen.

3. The test will stop at nine.

4. Take a step and stand there, Stacy.

5. Stan hit his chest with his fist.

6. Steve is stuck in the stove.

7. I am stuck in a state in the west.

8. Stay on the stool, Stan.

9. The staff will stop in the store.

1. speak	sped	spit	spike
2. spoon	spat	spine	spade
3. gasp	lisp	spin	spy
4. spell	spun	Spain	spook
5. spoke	spud	spill	speck

1. I spoke with a spy in Spain.

2. Please spell the word "spoon," Stan.

3. Spin the spoon on the table.

 4. Gasp! Don't spill the tea!

5. Speak to Spike, but don't yell.

Word List and Sentences

1. scoot	skate	scam	skit
2. school	sky	tusk	scale
3. scud	scab	scum	skid
4. sketch	scuff	skim	risk
5. task	scone	musk	Scott
6. skin	bask	skill	skiff

1. Scott will skate to school.

2. The scam is a big risk.

3. Stacy can sketch the sky with skill.

4. I have a scab on my skin.

Consonant Blends

BINGO

- Write **one word** from page **25 or 26** in each square below.
- When your teacher says a word, write an **X** on the word if you see it in a square.
- The first person to have **5 X's** in a row is the winner!

Consonant Blends

Review Quiz

Listen to the words your teacher says, and write the missing letter in the blanks.

(Answer key in the back of the book.)

1. s_ill

2. s_ack

3. B_ian

4. s_ab

5. p_an

6. c_ap

7. s_ay

8. s_oon

9. s_ate

10. f_ee

Listen to the sentences your teacher says, and fill in the missing letters.

1. S__an will s__op in the s__ore.

2. P__ease s__ell the word "b__oke."

3. B__ake has a ras__ on his s__in.

Consonant Blends – sm / sn

Word List and Sentences

1. smoke	snake	smack	snail
2. snow	smell	snack	smite
3. sneak	Smith	smile	snipe
4. snoop	smooth	smash	snatch
5. snag	smote	smooch	snitch

1. Smith will sneak by the snake.

2. He will smile when he sees a snail.

3. The snake's skin is not smooth.

4. I smell smoke! Rush to the snow!

5. The smell is just a fresh snack.

Consonant Blends – squ / sw

Word List and Sentences

1. swim   sweet   swill   Swiss
2. squeak   squeeze   squeak   squint
3. swell   squeal   sway   swipe
4. squid   swam   swing   square
5. squish   swish   squire   swum

1. Mice squeal and eat Swiss cheese.

2. The squid swims well.

3. He likes to swim in a square.

 4. Smith will squint in the sun.

5. Squeeze the fresh squid.

Review - Consonant Blends

1. scam   skate   spit   smoke
2. snack   squeak   stay   scab
3. skim   spell   smell   snake
4. squeeze   sweet   score   skate
5. speed   Smith   snow   squeal
6. stat   sketch   sped   smack
7. sneak   squint   swill   Swiss
8. spoon   smite   snail   scale

1. Smith eats Swiss cheese.

2. We sneak to the school and swim at night.

3. The quick snake ate my snack.

4. The snail's speed is quite slow.

Consonant Blends – Rhyming Words

Draw lines to match the rhyming words below.

snack	stay
pray	swim
squeeze	steed
skim	skit
stitch	stack
spit	sneeze
stain	switch
tweed	swoon
fry	train
spoon	sky

Tongue Twisters!

1. Six sticky sucker sticks.

2. I slit the sheet
   the sheet I slit
   and on this slitted sheet I sit.

 3. Freshly fried fresh flesh.

4. Try three free throws.

5. Brad's back bike brake broke.

6. Six thick thistle sticks.
   Six thick thistles stick.

7. Sam's shop stocks socks.

Consonant Blends with s

Review Quiz

Write the word your teacher says on the blanks below. (Answer key in the back of the book.)

1. _____   6. _____

2. _____   7. _____

3. _____   8. _____

4. _____   9. _____

5. _____   10. _____

Listen to the sentences your teacher says, and fill in the blanks with the missing words.

Stan can _____ the _____.

Quinn is a _____ girl.

There's a _____ on my _____.

Can you _____ to the _____?

*See page 48 for more reading practice.

Consonant Blends – scr / spl / str / spr

Word List

1. scratch	splash	stretch	spray
2. scrub	split	strap	spree
3. scram	strive	spry	scrap
4. splint	stray	sprite	scream
5. struck	screen	spleen	strip
6. scribe	splat	strife	screw
7. stress	sprain	scrip	sprint

Sentences

1. I see a strand on the screen.

2. Steve will sprint to school.

3. The stray dog will scratch and scratch.

4. Spray the stain and scrub.

5. I strive to sprint fast.

6. Fred will scrub the stray cat.

7. Try not to strip the screw.

8. Stress leads to strife.

Consonant Blends – thr vs. fr

Word List

*The sounds **thr** and **fr** sound very similar. Practice saying each sound, and listen for the different sounds.

1. throw   free   three   Fred

2. frail   thrown   freed   thrive

3. frame   Frank   thrill   frat

4. frost   throne   frog   thrust

5. fret   fresh   threw   freak

6. fry   thrift   throat   fruit

7. throb   frill   fright   freeze

1. Throw the frame to Fred.

2. Frank got a thrill and a fright.

3. The frog will thrill Frank.

4. Don't freeze the fresh fruit.

5. Fred threw a ball to Frank.

6. Those three frames are free.

7. Fred freed the frail frog.

8. Fruit can not thrive in frost.

Consonant Blends

Numbers Game

Rules (see introduction for more ways to play this game):

- Choose one student to say a word (any word) from below.
- The first student to **find the word** and **say the number** in the box gets to say the next word.

1 throw	2 show	3 sneeze	4 freeze	5 breed
6 thrill	7 frill	8 squeeze	9 flee	10 bleed
11 skill	12 still	13 strip	14 scrip	15 scream
16 plead	17 steed	18 freed	19 throes	20 stream
21 preen	22 free	23 three	24 scrap	25 strap

Consonant Blends

Spelling

Write the word your teacher says on the blanks below. (Answer key in the back of the book.)

1. _____   6. _____

2. _____   7. _____

3. _____   8. _____

4. _____   9. _____

5. _____   10. _____

Listen to the sentences your teacher says, and fill in the blanks with the missing words.

Don't _____ the _____ cat.

The scab will _____.

The _____ can _____.

_____ is a good _____.

Consonant Digraphs – ph

Word List

1. phone   graph   phase

2. phony   phones   photo

3. phonics   telephone phrases

4. humph   dolphin   elephant

5. hyphen   nephew   orphan

6. phase   Ralph   graphs

7. dolphins photos   phrase

Sentences

1. Read the phonics book.

2. Ralph has two phones.

3. The orphan has photos.

4. The graph is on the phone.

5. "Humph," said Ralph the orphan.

6. The graphs show a bad phase.

7. Look at the dolphins and elephants!

1. know	gnome	knew
2. knife	knee	gnat
3. sign	knob	kneel
4. knell	signs	knight
5. knit	knot	knock

1. The gnome knows the knight.

2. Ralph knits and kneels.

3. Knock on the sign.

4. The gnat is on the knob.

5. "Knock knock," said the knight.

1. write	wrist	wrote
2. wren	wreck	wrap
3. writ	wrong	wrath
4. wrench	wreath	Wright
5. wrinkle	wry	wrens

1. The wrens know how to fly.

2. Please hand me a wrench.

3. Why is your wrist in a wrap?

4. Wright can write with his wrist.

5. Stan wrote the wrong sign.

Consonant Blends – Rhyming Words

 Draw lines to match the rhyming words below.

phase	knit
writ	pine
sign	raise
splat	home
Wright	bite
strap	phone
moan	gnat
knee	strong
wrong	wrap
gnome	free

Consonant Blends – silent k / g, wr, ph

Spelling

Write the word your teacher says on the blanks below. (Answer key in the back of the book.)

1. _____   6. _____

2. _____   7. _____

3. _____   8. _____

4. _____   9. _____

5. _____   10. _____

Listen to the sentences your teacher says, and fill in the blanks with the missing words.

Use your _____ to write the _____.

The gnome _____ the _____.

_____ will _____ his car.

There's a _____ on your_____.

*See page 49-50 for more reading practice.

"Chad and Shaun"

Chad and Shaun play together every day after school. They like to race their bikes in the city; Chad will chase Shaun, then Shaun will chase Chad.

Sometimes, they go to the gym and play tennis or baseball. At night, they will rush home and chat on the Internet. Chad and Shaun are very good friends.

Reading Review

"Shane's Stain"

Shane likes to skate to school and listen to music. Today, when he came to class, he had a big **stain** on his shirt.

"Why do you have a big **stain** on your shirt, Shane?" asked his friend Steve.

"Because," said Shane. I spilled my juice when I was on my skates."

"Then next time don't drink juice when you skate!" said Steve.

Reading Review

"The Snake at the Lake"

One day, Ralph and his sister Gen took a walk to the lake. They sat in the shade and threw stones in the lake.
Splash! Splash!
"This is a nice day," said Ralph. "I'm glad we came to the lake."
"Me too-" said Gen, but then she screamed. *"Ahhhhh!"*

Ralph jumped up. "What's wrong?" he said.
"There's a snake! There's a snake!" screamed Gen.

Ralph saw the snake by the lake. "It's just a little snake," he said. "Don't shock me like that!"

"I know it's a little snake, but I don't like snakes. Throw a stone at the snake!"

"No way!" said Ralph. "If we leave the snake alone, it will leave us alone, too."

"Okay," said Gen, "but if the snake comes over here, I will run home right away!

Answer Key

Page 5
Part 1 – Words
1. mage
2. lice
3. gist
4. while
5. mace
6. whole
7. huge
8. rice
9. whack
10. sage

Part 2 – Fill in the blank
1. The genie is in a white cage.
2. Who can race on my bike?
3. Roll the dice on the page.
4. The giant has a whip. He is in a rage.

Page 16
Part 1 – Words
1. patch
2. wish
3. thud
4. sham
5. chick
6. faith
7. those
8. chum
9. shape
10. chop

Part 2 – Fill in the blank
1. I have a rash on my shin.
2. I will latch the window.
3. He has a thin gash on his chin.
4. There is a fish by the path.

Page 21
Part 1 – Words
1. flip
2. crass
3. prize
4. black
5. sled
6. grip
7. broke
8. plan
9. trade
10. glad

Part 2 – Fill in the blanks
1. Grace has a plan for the slum.
2. Trap the crab in the pen.
3. My brave friend got a prize.
4. The flock can flip and glide.

Page 28
Words
1. spill
2. stack
3. Brian
4. scab
5. plan
6. clap
7. stay
8. spoon
9. skate
10. free

Sentences
1. Stan will stop in the store.
2. Please spell the word "broke."
3. Blake has a rash on his skin.

Page 34
Part 1 – Words
1. skate
2. snack
3. spike
4. stab
5. squeal
6. swipe
7. smell
8. snide
9. stoke
10. slow

Part 2 – Fill in the blank
1. Stan can smell the snack.
2. Quinn is a sweet girl.
3. There's a scab on my skin.
4. Can you sneak to the school?

Page 40
Part 1 – Words
1. spleen
2. thrust
3. free
4. three
5. street
6. scrap
7. sprig
8. strap
9. spruce
10. splat

Part 2 – Fill in the blank
1. Don't throw the stray cat.
2. The scab will throb.
3. The sprite can spray.
4. Frank is a good scribe.

Page 46
Part 1 – Words
1. knife
2. wren
3. phase
4. sign
5. knit
6. phone
7. wrote
8. know
9. write
10. wrap

Part 2 – Fill in the blank
1. Use your wrist to write the phrase.
2. The gnome knew the graph.
3. Ralph will wreck his car.
4. There's a gnat on your knee.

2480458R00029

Made in the USA
San Bernardino, CA
26 April 2013